Essential Lives

AMY TAN

Essential Lives

AMY TAN
AUTHOR EXTRAORDINAIRE

by Tamra Orr

Content Consultant:
Malini Johar Schueller, PhD
Professor of English, University of Florida

ABDO
Publishing Company

CREDITS

Published by ABDO Publishing Company, 8000 West 78th Street, Edina, Minnesota 55439. Copyright © 2010 by Abdo Consulting Group, Inc. International copyrights reserved in all countries. No part of this book may be reproduced in any form without written permission from the publisher. The Essential Library™ is a trademark and logo of ABDO Publishing Company.

Printed in the United States.

Editor: Amy Van Zee
Copy Editor: Paula Lewis
Interior Design and Production: Emily Love
Cover Design: Emily Love

Library of Congress Cataloging-in-Publication Data
Orr, Tamra.
  Amy Tan : author extraordinaire / by Tamra Orr.
      p. cm. — (Essential lives)
  Includes bibliographical references and index.
  ISBN 978-1-60453-705-5
 1. Tan, Amy—Juvenile literature. 2. Novelists, American—20th century—Biography—Juvenile literature. 3. Chinese Americans—Biography—Juvenile literature. 4. Asian American authors—Biography—Juvenile literature. I. Title.

PS3570.A48Z8 2009
813'.54—dc22
[B]

2008055528

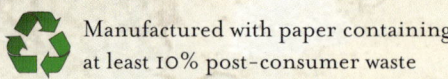
Manufactured with paper containing at least 10% post-consumer waste

Amy Tan

TABLE OF CONTENTS

Chapter 1	From Page to Stage	6
Chapter 2	Fitting In	16
Chapter 3	Growing Up	26
Chapter 4	Losing Loved Ones	36
Chapter 5	Purpose through Loss	48
Chapter 6	Becoming a Writer	58
Chapter 7	Turning a Corner	68
Chapter 8	Finding Joy	76
Chapter 9	Keeping Up, Looking Forward	86

Timeline	96
Essential Facts	100
Additional Resources	102
Glossary	104
Source Notes	106
Index	110
About the Author	112

Chapter 1

A scene from The Bonesetter's Daughter

From Page to Stage

As a young girl, Amy Tan did not aspire to be the writer of an opera. But on September 13, 2008, that is exactly what she was. That evening *The Bonesetter's Daughter* premiered at the

Amy Tan

War Memorial Opera House in San Francisco, California. The opera was based on Tan's novel of the same name, which was published in 2001.

While the lights dimmed and the crowd grew quiet, music from the orchestra began to float over the audience as the opera's prologue began. Onstage, Chinese dragons flew through the air. Out of an ethereal fog appeared three women, each wearing a silk, high-collared Chinese dress. The three women opened their mouths to sing the first vocal notes of the piece, and Tan's opera was under way.

Writing an Opera

Despite the success of her novels, writing the opera was not an easy task for Tan. It took Stephen Wallace, the opera's composer, nine months to convince Tan that her novel should be set to music. Wallace and Tan had become friends at an artists'

Ghosts Onstage

The storyline of *The Bonesetter's Daughter* opera follows three generations of women: Precious Auntie, LuLing, and Ruth. Precious Auntie and LuLing were born in China, but Ruth was born in the United States. For much of the opera, Precious Auntie appears onstage as a ghost who leads Ruth back to China, while the story tells of what happened to Ruth's mother, LuLing.

Opera Publicity

Tan enjoyed the process of turning her novel into an opera. Not only was a book written about the process, but a documentary film was also written for public television and chronicled the progress of bringing the opera to the stage.

colony in New York in the 1990s. Tan was unfamiliar with the process of making an opera, but Wallace saw the potential in her story. Tan and Wallace even traveled together to China to research the opera, witnessing Chinese festivals and celebrations to help compose the music and lyrics.

Once Tan found her writing routine, the opera began to take shape. As Wallace said, "She was completely intuitive about what needed to be done."[1] Once the opera was written and rehearsals began, Tan was directly involved with the production. She even found her mother's old mink coat to provide the actors with inspiration for a particular scene.

After the opera's debut, reviewers praised the opera not only for its creative vision, costumes, and singers, but also for the collaboration between Wallace and Tan—between

Tan lives in San Francisco, California, and in New York City.

music and story. Joshua Kosman, a writer for the *San Francisco Chronicle*, wrote that the opera was a "rare creation—a new opera in which musical characterization, dramatic clarity and theatrical vigor combine to form an arresting and vividly memorable experience."[2] At the premiere, both Wallace and Tan were given a prolonged standing ovation.

Art Imitating Life

As a writer of novels, short stories, and essays dealing mainly with women and Chinese culture, Tan has pleased readers around the world. Her work has been translated into more than 35 languages. Beginning with her first published novel, *The Joy Luck Club*, in 1989, Tan has fascinated her fans with characters that struggle to balance their family traditions with life in a modern world. Herself a daughter of Chinese immigrants, Tan weaves memories of her own childhood into the lives of her characters.

Many claim that Tan's stories are so powerful because parts of them are based on something from Tan's life.

A Published Author

In addition to short stories and essays, Tan has written the following books:
- *The Joy Luck Club*, 1989
- *The Kitchen God's Wife*, 1991
- *The Hundred Secret Senses*, 1995
- *The Bonesetter's Daughter*, 2001
- *The Opposite of Fate: A Book of Musings*, 2003
- *Saving Fish from Drowning*, 2005

Amy Tan

For example, Tan writes about female characters who feel pressure from their parents to succeed. Tan's parents put a great amount of pressure on her when she was a student, so she knows how to describe what her characters are experiencing.

If her characters contain some elements of her own life, however, how can a reader discern where the line ends between author and story? Literary critics of Tan claim that her own life "blurs the boundaries between fact and fiction."[3] Yet, Tan's personal experiences are what make her novels so

---

The Opposite of Fate

Tan's book of memories, *The Opposite of Fate: A Book of Musings*, is a collection of smaller pieces of writing. Some of these pieces have been previously published in magazines and newspapers such as *Harper's Bazaar*, the *New York Times*, and the *New Yorker*, among others.

The first piece in the book was written in part because Tan wanted to clear up some misunderstandings. One day, she wandered into a bookstore and found a *CliffsNotes* book on *The Joy Luck Club*. The *CliffsNotes* author implied that Tan had embedded deep symbolic meanings into her texts, and Tan was stunned. Tan had written a story, and the literary dissection of her book provided meanings that she had not necessarily intended. She wrote the essay to assure her readers that she did not write complex stories meant to confuse; she wrote stories as a way of processing her life.

Many of the essays in the book are humorous views of things that have happened to Tan since she became an author, including the difficulty she had in writing her second novel, *The Kitchen God's Wife*. *The Opposite of Fate* shows a very personal side of Tan, as well as displays her sense of humor and deep humility about herself as a writer.

captivating. As a young girl, Tan struggled in her relationship with her Chinese-born mother, Daisy. Many of Tan's novels focus on mother-daughter relationships that have their own sets of highs and lows. It is clear that the characters are crafted with love and affection, perhaps because they are modeled after one of Tan's loved ones, or even Tan herself.

In *The Opposite of Fate: A Book of Musings*, Tan compares her writing process to the creation of a quilt. In attempting to deal with her own personal trials, writing became the outlet she needed to process the difficulties of her life. She also found that when she would write fiction stories, she had plenty of experiences that served as research and made her stories much more realistic. Tan writes, "It is a crazy quilt of love, pieced together, torn apart, repaired again and again, and strong enough to protect us all."[4]

A Successful Career

The literary community has praised Tan for addressing the stereotypes of Asian Americans head-on. Particularly in her essays and memoirs from childhood, Tan frankly discusses the difficulty she had understanding and getting along with her

Amy Tan

Chinese mother. At a time when Tan was trying to fit in with her peers, her mother often embarrassed Tan with her Chinese accent and bold speech. Yet, these themes of "identity crisis" are what make Tan's literature so endearing. Tan is candid about the meshing of old and new, East and West, and family generations, which are relevant themes to many readers today.

In U.S. literature, Tan represents a voice that speaks for thousands of people. By bringing the struggles of Asian Americans and other minority groups to light, Tan's fiction provides much food for thought. She is well respected by many for her discernment, creativity, and literary taste. In addition to her writing, she joined the *Los Angeles Times* in 2006 as Literary Editor of its Sunday magazine, *West*.

So what was Tan's childhood like? What instances from her upbringing

Featuring California

West, the *Los Angeles Times*' Sunday magazine, was launched on February 5, 2006. As Literary Editor, Tan is responsible for selecting short fiction pieces for the "California Story" section, which features short stories that are set in the state. Other features of the magazine include photographs, cartoons, California history, and a crossword puzzle.

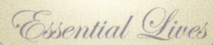

provided ideas for her plotlines? Like the characters in her novels, Tan's early years were filled with love, confusion, and struggle. And like many young people today, Tan set her hopes high and worked through the difficulties.

Amy Tan

Tan spoke at The New Yorker Festival in 2002.

Chapter 2

Amy Tan as an infant with her mother, Daisy

FITTING IN

Amy stared at herself in the mirror. No matter which way she turned or from what angle she looked, there was no doubt about it: she looked Chinese. She may have been born in

Amy Tan

Oakland, California, but she looked every bit as Chinese as her mother and father, who had both been born in China. Her Chinese name was An-Mei, which meant "blessing from America."

She did not feel like any kind of blessing. Leaning closer, she looked at her nose. Amy wished that here nose were long and thin like an American's. Suddenly, she had an idea. She ran into the kitchen, grabbed a clothespin, and clamped it onto her nose. It pinched terribly, but it was tolerable. Maybe if she wore this clothespin to bed every night for at least a week, it would reshape her nose, she thought.

Feeling Like an Outsider

Amy Tan, one of today's most well-known authors, was born in 1952. Even though she was born in America, her distinct Chinese features made her feel like an

Assimilation

One of Amy's biggest struggles growing up was figuring out how to deal with being a person of Chinese descent living in the United States. One of her frustrations was that her teachers often tried to steer her toward math and science courses, as if her teachers somehow thought that her English was poor because of her Chinese heritage.

outsider at school. Her almond-shaped eyes and jet-black hair made her stand out among the blue-eyed, blonde-haired students surrounding her. The differences did not stop there. She heard the insults the other kids made whenever they saw her mother, Daisy, and heard her accent and the sound of her rapid-fire Chinese.

The others' laughter made Amy feel angry and sad at the same time. She felt as if she lived a life with her feet in two different worlds. During the day, she went to school, spoke English, and did everything she

---

San Francisco's Chinatown

Although there are a number of "Chinatowns" scattered across the country, the Chinatown in San Francisco is the oldest, largest, and most well-known of them all. Some of Amy's characters live in or near the San Francisco Chinatown. In the middle of the nineteenth century, when gold was discovered in California, many Chinese laborers flocked to the state to find work. Chinese began migrating in growing numbers to northern California. Like many immigrants throughout history, they came in search of jobs, money, and a second chance at life. But these Chinese laborers were often the victims of racial discrimination. The Chinese Exclusion Act of 1882 limited labor immigration.

Under the exclusionary laws, Chinese immigrants banded together to form businesses and cultural undertakings of their own. These communities, however, also added to the view of Chinese people as outsiders, because they joined together under their similar heritage but lived separately from the rest of society.

Today, San Francisco's Chinatown is considered one of the most popular tourist attractions in the area. Visitors buy souvenirs, but they also can discover the rich heritage and history of the unique area.

could to fit in with her American classmates. She and her brothers, John and Peter, embraced this Western culture as much as they could, pushing their foreign heritage behind them whenever possible. During the evenings and weekends, however, the three of them only spoke Chinese, ate Chinese food, and spent all their time with their parents and their Chinese neighbors and friends. Amy felt as if it were a double life.

Embarrassment

Amy had a difficult time forgetting one particular night in her home. The local minister had been invited for dinner, along with his handsome, blonde, teenage son Robert. Amy had a crush on Robert. "When I found out that my parents had invited the minister's family over for Christmas dinner, I cried," she recalls in her essay "Fish Cheeks."

In Love with San Francisco

Amy Tan has spent most of her life living in the San Francisco, California, area. She appreciates the diversity of the city and enjoys the variety of activities. In San Francisco, one can go hiking and then, within a short period of time, be downtown watching an opera. "This city is like an opera—very dramatic, historical, tragic, funny, lyrical, beautiful, over-the-top," she says.[1]

Traditional Chinese dishes include fish and other seafood.

"What would Robert think of our shabby Chinese Christmas?"² She struggled to get through the meal of tofu, squid, dried fungus, and other uniquely Chinese dishes. It seemed as if the guests looked at the food with disgust. Amy was embarrassed about herself, her family, and most of all, her Chinese heritage. It took a long time before she realized why

Amy Tan

her mother had chosen those exact recipes.

> *It wasn't until many years later—long after I had gotten over my crush on Robert—that I was able to appreciate fully her lesson and the true purpose behind our particular menu. For Christmas Eve that year, she had chosen all my favorite foods.*³

Strangely enough, it would be the same heritage that Amy was so desperately trying to escape that would bring her both fame and fortune later in life. In writing about the stories of her ancestors and their homeland, she would not only become a best-selling author, but would also come to terms with a culture that she spent most of her young life fighting to ignore.

An Isolated Childhood

Amy's childhood was much like any other young person's. She spent

"Dinner threw me deeper into despair. My relatives licked the ends of their chopsticks and reached across the table, dipping into the dozen or so plates of food. Robert and his family waited patiently for platters to be passed to them. My relatives murmured with pleasure when my mother brought out the whole steamed fish. Robert grimaced. Then my father poked his chopsticks just below the fish eye and plucked out the soft meat. 'Amy, your favorite,' he said, offering me the tender fish cheek. I wanted to disappear."⁴

—Amy Tan, from "Fish Cheeks"

a lot of time riding her bike, going to the library, mowing the lawn, and watching and interacting with nature. Amy's parents struggled to find the place where they felt they fit the best, so the family often moved from one community to another in northern California. This only made the quest to fit in more difficult. Just as Amy would start to make a friend, the family would move—sometimes almost every year.

Looking back, Amy believes moving so often made her feel more alone and isolated than she might have otherwise. She spent a lot of time writing letters to the few friends she left behind. Because she thought her life was quite dull, she made up most of the material in her letters. But she also credits her mobile lifestyle with giving her a great tool that helped her later in life as a writer: observation. In her early years of feeling like an outsider, Amy honed the observational skills that helped her write such detailed characters. Eventually, the family settled down in Santa Clara, California.

Finding Literature

While Amy loved her parents—and they loved her—things were not always calm and quiet in their household. Reflecting on her life, Amy wrote,

Amy Tan

> *I remember that starting at the age of six, I had thoughts of suicide. . . . The fact that I had those thoughts when I was very young was an indication that I was a very gloomy kid. I had some ways of thinking that were not healthy.*⁵

Amy found her best escape and her best answers to life's questions through reading. Reading was a refuge for her, and a place where she could use her imagination to create the life she had always wanted but had never experienced. In stories, she could find happiness by becoming one of the characters. From her earliest years, Amy possessed a creative mind and an insatiable appetite for books.

The combination of being pulled by two different cultures, a rocky relationship with her mother, and a drive to escape into a book created an Amy Tan that would turn into one of the nation's most beloved writers of

A World of Reading

Since Amy found such an escape in reading, she spent a lot of time with a book in her hands. She loved fairy tales, especially the grim and gruesome ones. She also enjoyed the rhythm and style of Bible stories. She was a fan of Laura Ingalls Wilder's *Little House on the Prairie* books and read all of them. By the age of ten, she was reading *To Kill a Mockingbird*, even though, as she said, it had a lot of big words in it. Reading higher-level books made her feel more grown up as well, which was something she longed to be.

multilayered characters. These fascinating characters often echoed elements of the author's life, making their stories realistic, sympathetic, and dramatic.

Amy Tan

Some of Amy Tan's stories take place near Chinatown in San Francisco, California.

Chapter 3

Amy's parents, John and Daisy, in China in 1945

Growing Up

Many of the most important characters that fill the pages of Amy Tan's stories and novels are born from the tales her parents told her of life in China. The lessons learned by her ancestors and the advice and adventures of generations of relatives pop up in her various plots and themes. It is easy to understand why, as her family background is rich with history.

Her father, John Tan, was an electrical engineer and Baptist minister. Born in China in 1913, he was the oldest of 12 children. In the 1940s, he met a married woman named Daisy. Daisy had seen her own mother, Jing Mei, die in front of her. Jing Mei had eaten a cake that she herself had filled with poison. It was a tragedy that would affect Daisy's ability to mother. "My mother had a very difficult childhood having seen her own mother kill herself," recalled Tan. "So she didn't always know how to be the nurturing mother that we all expect we should have."[1]

John and Daisy fell in love and had an affair. Daisy's husband was an abusive man, and she soon sought a divorce. She lost custody of her three daughters and was thrown into prison for her adultery. When Daisy was imprisoned, John did not know what to do. He came to the United States in 1947 to study at the Massachusetts Institute of Technology (MIT). He arrived in San Francisco and soon realized that MIT was not the right pathway for him. John Tan stayed in San Francisco and went to divinity school instead. All his brothers and sisters were ministers. He knew it was the right choice for himself as well.

When Daisy was released from prison two years later, she sent a telegram to John in California. She told him she was free and asked him if he still wanted to be with her. Should she come to him in the United States? He said yes. Daisy managed to escape from China on the last boat leaving Shanghai before the 1949 Communist takeover. She was not allowed to take her children with her. She and John were soon reunited. They married and became parents of Peter, Amy, and John.

Meeting Expectations

John and Daisy Tan certainly wanted the best for their children, as most parents do. Sometimes they demonstrated this desire in ways that put intense pressure on their

---

MIT

John Tan received a scholarship to attend MIT before giving it up for a career in ministry instead. Founded in 1861, MIT is located in Boston, Massachusetts, and specializes in science and technology.

Today, more than 10,000 undergraduates and graduates are enrolled. The school is quite difficult to get into, only accepting 12.5 percent of the students who apply, and is known for producing a number of Nobel Prize winners.

children, even at an early age. They had extremely high expectations of Amy and wanted her to bring home perfect grades, even in kindergarten. In her kindergarten class, Amy had carefully drawn a picture of a house with a chimney, windows, and trees around it. Another girl drew a more abstract picture, but the other girl's picture was chosen to be displayed in the principal's office. Daisy wanted to know why Amy's picture was not selected for the principal's office. Amy felt pressure to excel in all areas of school from a very young age.

There was no doubt what the Tans wanted for their daughter Amy: she was to become both a doctor and a concert pianist. Those were the options, regardless of whether they were Amy's interests—which they were not. What Amy really wanted to be was an artist, though she recognized that it was not typically a profession that earned much money. She wrote,

Influences

As a Baptist minister, John Tan had a strong influence on Amy. She saw his sermons as a method of storytelling. Her mother was also known for her stories of life in China, but she always told them in Chinese to relatives as she snapped beans at the table. Amy did find out that her family has a rich history of storytelling. One grandfather was an editor in China. Her other grandfather was a minister who wrote many sermons. "None of this was in English and they weren't writers of fiction, yet I think the written word was very much validated in my family," she stated in an interview.[2]

John, Daisy, Peter, and Amy Tan in Oakland, California, in 1952

My parents told me I would become a doctor and then in my spare time I would become a concert pianist. . . . It terrified me when I got to wondering if that was something I really could do. I wasn't that good a pianist and I didn't know if I really wanted to help people who were sick and had diseases. I didn't know if that was really in me, let alone if I could pass a science course.[3]

This constant pressure made Amy often feel that no matter how hard she tried, she could not live up to her parents' expectations. She felt that regardless of what she accomplished in life, she would never be able to make her parents proud. Like most young people, she longed for praise and acceptance from the most important people in her life. When she did not always receive praise from her parents, it made it difficult for her to deal with the constant pressure.

School Time

Amy loved school, but was drawn to words and letters far more than numbers and equations. "Words to me were magic. You could say a word and it could conjure up all kinds of images or feelings. . . . It was amazing to me that words had this power," she said.[4] Words would play an important role throughout her life.

Censorship

Because Tan has spent so much of her life as a reader and an author, she has a very strong feeling against the idea of censorship or book burning. A staunch advocate for the freedom of speech and the freedom of expression, Tan warns against the danger of banning any book. As she once wrote, "The danger is in creating the idea that somebody else is going to define the purpose of literature and confine who has access to it."[5]

Books were another way that Amy could find joy at a young age. She read a book a day, usually from the library. The only books in her household were Chinese fairy tales, Bibles, medical textbooks, a few secondhand novels, and the encyclopedia. By reading, she felt as though she could escape from anything she did not like in her own life. Books gave her the opportunity to use her imagination to become anyone she wanted to be in the story.

She did not let her parents know of her passion for reading, however. She was scared that if they found out, they would take the

First Time in Print

When she was eight years old, Amy wrote for a citywide contest and won. Her prize was a transistor radio and publication in the Santa Rosa *Press Democrat*. In describing her piece, Amy said she was trying hard to imitate her minister father. She wanted to be sincere and show how the library was her friend, because she really did feel that way. With the publication of her essay, it was the first time that Amy actually realized that writing could earn money. In a portion of the essay, Amy wrote,

My name is Amy Tan, 8 years old, a third grader in Matanzas School. It is a brand new school and everything is so nice and pretty. I love school because the many things I learn seem to turn on a light in the little room in my mind. I can see a lot of things I have never seen before. I can read many interesting books by myself now. I love to read. My father takes me to the library every two weeks, and I check five or six books each time. These books seem to open many windows in my little room. I can see many wonderful things outside. I always look forward to go [to] the library.[6]

books away from her. All this reading helped fuel her imagination, and looking back, she believes that the time spent immersed in books was the beginning of her writing career. She was always making up stories in her mind, and reading helped her come up with new ideas, new characters, and new ways to connect them.

Although books were limited in her home, stories were not. Her family engaged in quite a bit of storytelling. This included family stories, local gossip, and what happened to the people they had left behind in China. As her aunt and mother shelled peas over the newspaper-lined dining room table, they would talk nonstop in Shanghainese and Mandarin. Amy loved overhearing things that they thought she did not understand.

A Creative Mind

Amy was an excellent student and was advanced enough in her classes that she often found herself bored. Her third-grade teacher understood what she was going through and suggested that the school put her in a higher grade. Instead of promoting her, however, her parents decided to leave her in third grade. For that entire year, because she already knew

Inspiration at Home

Tan told the story of her grandmother in one of her novels. Some family members felt that revealing these family secrets was a betrayal. One relative was upset because she felt that the story of Tan's grandmother being raped, forced to become a concubine, and then committing suicide was a family secret that should not have been revealed.

Surprisingly, it was Tan's mother, Daisy, who came to her defense because Daisy had been forced to carry this shame all her life. Tan's grandmother had suffered in silence as well. According to Daisy, it was not too late to let the world know what had happened. Tan took comfort in this defense and let it guide her in her writing.

all the material, her teacher allowed her to spend time alone drawing pictures. Amy wrote,

> *So I had hours and hours of time where I was just left to my own devices . . . and she would encourage me. That was a wonderful period in my life. I mean, I didn't become an artist, but somebody let me do something I loved. What a luxury, to do something you love to do.*[7]

Amy's passion for words and stories stayed with her, but it would be years before she actually considered the possibility of using them as a career. Before that happened, she had to endure and learn from some major life changes.

Amy Tan

When she was eight years old, Amy Tan won an essay contest. Her essay was published in a local newspaper.

Chapter
4

Amy Tan at age 12 holding her cat, Fufu

Losing Loved Ones

Varying beliefs existed in the Tan household. Amy's father, a Baptist minister, was devoted to his faith. He encouraged Amy to believe in miracles and that God would take care of her. Amy enjoyed reading Bible stories, especially those that dealt with raising the dead to life and other miraculous events. Amy's mother, Daisy, declared a belief in God—when she was around her husband. Daisy had gone to a Catholic school in China. In addition to her Christian beliefs, Daisy also held some Buddhist beliefs, which included ancestor worship, ghosts, and curses.

Life changed suddenly in 1967 for the Tan family. Amy's father and older brother, Peter, were both diagnosed with brain tumors. Amy had held on to the Baptist beliefs her father had taught her and had been quite involved in the church. She truly believed that a miracle would happen: her brother and father would both live.

But soon, Amy's faith in God was beginning to fade. Her brother and father died within a year of each other, in 1967 and 1968. Tan later remembered,

> *Being 15 years old, I was at that ripe age when I would become a cynic about anything. So religion was the prime thing for me to reject. And I had all the reasons to reject it. When I lost my father and my brother, I realized I could not trust in any set of beliefs or absolute truths that had simply been handed to me. I had to ask questions too.*[1]

Essential Lives

Peter's Mistake

Amy's brother, Peter, was a straight-A student. He had done so well in school that he was set to graduate by the age of 16. When he wrote an essay for his English class, a friend asked if he could look at it in order to see how to write his own. Instead of doing that, the friend copied the essay word for word. The teacher failed both Peter and his friend—not just for the essay but for the entire semester. Peter was devastated and went into a deep depression. Then, just a few months later, he began having serious headaches. Days later, he started having convulsions and was finally diagnosed with a brain tumor. For the rest of her life, Daisy believed that the incident at school was what caused the tumor to grow in Peter's brain.

The family's doctor told Amy's mother that what had happened was just "bad luck." After the death of her husband, Daisy stopped praying to God and attempted to communicate with the ghosts of her past—her mother and now her husband John and son Peter. She sometimes asked Amy to use a Ouija board to talk with the spirits of ancestors and relatives.

Amy also struggled with her faith. She did not understand her mother's transition to Chinese customs. "The beliefs that my mother had, particularly in ghosts, were kept hidden from me and she didn't speak about them in the family until after my father died," she later explained.[2]

Moving On

As the sole parent now, Daisy felt she had to do something to rescue the rest of her family before evil spirits could claim their lives as well. She announced that she,

Amy Tan

Feng shui consultants use a compass to determine the best direction to face when sleeping, working, and relaxing.

John, and Amy were going to move immediately. She told her children that something bad occurred in their house, but nine bad things had already happened in their neighborhood. Daisy consulted a Chinese geomancer, who analyzed the good and bad "energies" in the Tan home. Geomancers analyze how these energies affect humans. Parts of this analysis are included in the Chinese art of feng shui. Because of the geomancer, Daisy felt that there were bad energies in their home in California, and the family had to get away immediately. Although Amy and her younger brother thought their mother was crazy, they did like the idea of moving and starting over.

The journey the Tan family took was long, exhausting, and filled with adventure. It was also a journey that Amy would long remember—especially for the confession that she heard from her mother during that time. Daisy finally

> **Feng Shui**
>
> Feng shui is an ancient Chinese art and literally means wind and water. It deals with life forces and energies, called chi, that are influenced by the arrangement of an environment.
>
> The practice of feng shui deals with the natural elements in the world and the belief that each of these elements has a life force. Those who practice feng shui believe that if the elements are unbalanced, it can result in disorder and cause stress. The balance of these forces is the goal of feng shui.
>
> Feng shui seeks to improve these chi energies to create a peaceful and harmonious environment. Those who practice feng shui believe that a properly arranged environment can increase a person's health, mood, and productivity.
>
> Feng shui has been practiced in China for more than 3,000 years. The art gained popularity in the United States in the late twentieth century. Feng shui is often applied to homes or office buildings. This can involve selecting colors, the placement of furniture, and the inclusion of natural elements into a space, such as fish tanks and potted plants. Today, consultants and authors write and discuss the art, offering advice on harmonious arrangements.

told her children of her first marriage in China and how she lost contact with her three daughters. It was a sobering moment for everyone. The realization of what her mother must have gone through stayed with Amy. These themes later found their way into her writing.

But the confession also scared Amy. When she heard about her half sisters, she felt threatened by them. She thought her mother had found a way to replace her because she had three more daughters who were Chinese. Amy was frightened that since her mother had left her first family, she might leave Amy as well.

First, the Tans traveled to New York, Washington DC, and Florida. They went across the Atlantic Ocean to the Netherlands. Daisy thought that the Netherlands was a clean place and would be suitable for her family. The family kept moving from one small city to another. They then took the train to Germany. From there they traveled from place to place in a Volkswagen, while Daisy searched for a new home and an American school for her two children. The family traveled for about a month until they eventually settled in Montreux, Switzerland, a beautiful city located on Lake Geneva.

There, Amy found a whole new persona—a much more reckless, rebellious one. For the first time, Amy was seen as exotic and desirable, and she began getting attention from men. It was very exciting to her. About being in Europe, Amy later said,

> *And there, away from everybody, away from the past, away from people who always thought I was this nerdy little girl, I exploded into a wild thing. I shortened my skirts, I put on makeup, I hung out with hippies.*[3]

Clearly, this new behavior upset Daisy as her daughter continued to rebel.

First Love

In 1968, Amy started dating a German man named Franz. Franz was about ten years older than Amy, and her mother strongly disapproved of him. Franz had an illegitimate

One or the Other

In an interview, Amy was asked to list the most important moments in her life. She replied, "Conflicts. Tragedies in life. Difficulties. A mother who was depressed. A father and brother who died. Being the only Chinese girl in a school. Moving every year. Graduating from a private school in Switzerland among rich people and not being rich. You know, those are the things that make you either psychotic or a fiction writer."[4]

child, friends who experimented with drugs, and he had escaped from a German army mental hospital.

"My mother was convinced that this man was going to ruin me," said Amy. "I knew he was pretty low. But it was pretty exciting. You know, first romance. This guy wrote beautiful love poetry and I just wanted somebody to think I was special at that age."[5]

Amy also wanted to prove that she could be "the baddest of the bad. I couldn't wait until I could leave the house. I thought, 'I'll divorce myself from this family and never see [Daisy] again.'"[6]

Amy's mother was in a panic. How could she stop her daughter from seeing this man? She became desperate. She yelled at Amy and even locked her in the bedroom. Daisy also became violent. She spoke of killing herself so that she would not have to see Amy ruin her life by dating Franz. The situation at home was tense.

Things went from bad to worse. Following another argument, Daisy entered Amy's room and locked the door. She was armed. "I saw the flash of a meat cleaver just before she pushed me to the wall and brought the blade's edge to within an inch of my throat," wrote Amy in her essay "Confessions."

Her eyes were like a wild animal's, shiny, fixated on the kill. In an excited voice, she said, "First, I kill you. Then Didi and me, our whole family destroy!" She smiled, her chest heaving. "Why don't you cry?" She pressed the blade closer and I could feel her breath gusting.[7]

For almost 15 minutes, mother and daughter stayed in this position. Amy finally began crying and said she wanted to live.

Dangerous Behavior

Despite the feud within Amy's household, it was not long before Amy began engaging in behaviors that were even more risky. She was socializing with people who were completely alien to her. Soon she was smoking and drinking. Finally, a dramatic event made Amy turn her life around.

In an act of desperation, Daisy hired a private detective to keep an

High School

Amy attended the Institut Monte Rosa Internationale High School—a college prep school—located in Territet/Montreux, Switzerland. It was founded in 1874 to help high school age students prepare themselves for college. Students prepare to take College Board exams. Classes are also designed for those who plan on entering business colleges. A one-year post-graduate program offers a focus on language study, business, economics, and computer studies.

eye on Amy and her boyfriend. Daisy gave the detective Amy's diary, which contained all the information he needed to initiate a drug raid. With the information, the authorities found marijuana in a van that belonged to some of Franz's friends. Franz and his friends were deported.

Amy admits that a part of her attraction to Franz was rebellion, but the tension between mother and daughter had become so intense it was making Amy physically sick. Looking back, Amy says that she did a lot of things out of anger, but as time went on, things started to get better between her and her mother. Amy decided to make a new start.

It was time for Amy to get her life together, and that is exactly what she did. First, she graduated from Switzerland's Institut Monte Rosa Internationale High School in 1969. Then, her family made the decision to return to the United States and

Linfield College

Amy spent a brief time at Linfield College, located in McMinnville, Oregon. Originally chartered in 1858, the four-year college is affiliated with American Baptist Churches USA. Today, 1,700 students are enrolled. The college focuses on the liberal arts and sciences. Although religion commitment is not required to attend, the school does offer faith-based student groups and a Religious Studies department.

moved to San Francisco. Soon after, Amy enrolled in Linfield College, a Baptist university in Oregon, which her mother had selected for her.

 Amy's rebellious moments were not gone, however. After only two semesters at Linfield, she quit and transferred to San Jose City College. She had met a tax law attorney on a blind date and was in love again. This time, however, would be different.

Amy Tan

Montreux, Switzerland, where the Tan family lived

Chapter 5

Louis DeMattei and Amy Tan in 1974

Purpose through Loss

When Tan began dating Franz in Germany, her mother put a stop to it as swiftly as possible. Now, Tan was making another decision about her life that her mother strongly disagreed with. However, this time, there was nothing Daisy could do about it. In 1971, Tan left Linfield College and a pre-med curriculum to follow her new love—an Italian American named Louis DeMattei. She decided to major in English and linguistics and transferred from San Jose City College to San Jose State University. Daisy was not happy and did not speak to her for six months.

The silence and separation were difficult for both of them. Tan was grateful that she had a partner to share it with. On April 6, 1974, she and DeMattei were married. Tan stated,

> *I was lucky that I met a very kind person, a very good person and that person is now my husband. He is a very sweet man. I wasn't in love with him when I first met him, but I knew he was a good person. I said, "This is the kind of person my father was." Four years later, I married Lou and we have been together ever since. . . . He's been my stability in life.*[1]

As Tan worked on getting her college degree, she held a number of odd jobs, including working as a telephone switchboard operator, a carhop, a bartender, and a pizza maker. Eventually, she earned a bachelor's and then a master's degree in linguistics from San Jose State University. She studied for a doctorate at the University of California at Berkeley, although she withdrew from the program in 1976.

While she was in the program, she suffered another tragic loss in her life.

The Loss of a Friend

Tan and DeMattei shared an apartment with a Berkeley bioengineering student named Pete (Tan does not include his last name in her writing, in order to respect him). The three of them were good friends, spending hours in deep philosophical conversations, as well as going on backpacking trips together.

One night, Pete told his friends about a dream he had in which strangers broke into his room and slowly strangled

A Perfect Date

While Tan was living in Oregon and attending Linfield College, she went on a blind date with Louis DeMattei. At first, she thought that the relationship would be brief—not anything important. Soon after, however, they went out again, this time on a hot August afternoon to San Juan Bautista, an old city in California's San Juan Valley. It was a town that was deeply steeped in the past. Filled with an old mission and buildings with false fronts, it spoke of old stories and ghostly visitors.

After exploring and hiding in corners for kisses, Tan and DeMattei ran into a wedding being held in an old dance hall. The wedding couple immediately invited the two of them to join in the celebration. For hours, they danced to the sounds of a mariachi band, singing along and shouting. When the party finally broke up, the two of them went outside to lie on the grass and rest for a moment. They arrived just in time to see a breathtaking Perseid meteor shower, in which meteors streak through the night sky every few minutes. It was at that moment, said Tan, that both of them recognized that they were indeed in love.

him. His fears were not completely unfounded. The three friends had recently experienced death threats made against them by a local gang after they had a run-in at a local pizza restaurant. A fistfight ensued, in which Pete broke the nose of one gang member. Although the police were aware of the threats, they could not do anything about the situation. The three roommates decided it might be safest to split up into two apartments in another neighborhood. Pete found another apartment in a different building. The three of them all slept in Pete's apartment the first night.

The next morning was Tan's twenty-fourth birthday. She and DeMattei spent the evening eating out and visiting friends. Pete stayed behind because he had a cold. The next day, Tan and DeMattei found that Pete's earlier nightmare had been more of a premonition. Two people had broken into his new place and tied him up. He was slowly strangled. DeMattei and Tan were called in to identify the body. In her essay, "A Question of Fate," Tan wrote,

> Since then, whenever I read stories of wars, earthquakes, or murders, I have imagined those who have seen what I have, the face of a loved one, not in peaceful slumber as morticians

A view of the University of California-Berkeley campus, where Tan studied for a doctorate in linguistics

might have devised, but as it appeared at the moment of death, a body unwashed, ungroomed, not prepared, in any conceivable way, to be viewed by another human being, let alone someone who loved that person.[2]

A few days later, Tan was with some friends mourning Pete's death. Suddenly, she blurted out that the names of Pete's killers were Ronald and John. Tan claimed that Pete had told her the names. Not long after, two men were arrested for the murder—and their names were Ronald and John.

To this day, Tan feels that Pete is near her, giving her advice and guidance. She credits him with being the inspiration she needed to leave the doctoral program before she was done and focus on a new interest: working with developmentally disabled children. When he had first suggested it, a few months before he died, she had responded negatively. She did not particularly like children. That was his field, not hers.

A Change in Attitude

After Pete's death, however, her attitude changed and she interviewed for a job working with challenged children. It was immediately clear that Tan was not the right person for the job. Tan stood up to leave when suddenly she heard Pete's voice in her head. He was encouraging her to tell the interviewer the reason she was there.

Dealing with Death

For the seven years following Pete's death, on Tan's birthday, she lost her voice for psychological reasons. She felt it was a reflection of the horror she had seen and could not talk about.

I heard Pete telling me that I should simply tell this woman my motivations in applying for a job with exactly these challenges and unknowns. And out came my story of Pete's death and my pledge to do with my life what he had intended to do with his. Ten minutes later, I was hired.[3]

From 1976 to 1981, Tan worked as a language development consultant for Alameda County Association for Retarded Citizens in Oakland. She worked with children with autism, Down syndrome, and cerebral palsy from birth to age five. In this position, she observed kids closely and then assessed them for their various skill levels. After that, Tan worked with the children's parents and teachers to help create a specific plan for each case. The children taught her a great deal about life and compassion. Amy stated,

What Is Important

Because of the loss of her father and brother when she was young, as well as her friend Pete later in life, Tan spends a lot of time thinking about death. Tan hopes that whatever and wherever afterlife is, the people she loves will be there. She finds that thinking about these ideas helps keep things in balance.

With the kids themselves, I learned to play, to discover what made them laugh, what they could not resist watching or touching or reaching for. I found myself observing not deficits but the qualities of souls. . . . It was the best training I could have had for becoming a writer.[4]

As time went by, Tan also had more time to reflect on her emotionally charged relationship with her mother. She realized that Daisy, like all other humans, was not perfect. Her actions always sprung from love for her daughter. That did not make them the best or right decisions, but the intentions were full of love for her. "Once I realized that and stopped taking it as a personal attack to torture me and make my life miserable," wrote Tan, "then I could look beyond it. I could even look at it with some humor eventually."[5] Slowly, Tan and her mother began communicating again.

Taking Time to Listen

Later in life, Tan took the time to sit down and record much of her mother's life story. It was a rewarding experience for both of them. "I realized that I had never really listened in the way she wanted someone to," Tan said. "She wanted someone to go back and relive her life with her. It was a way for her to exorcize her demons, and for me to finally listen and empathize and learn what memory means, and what you can change about the past. She's a wonderful storyteller, for observation of character, emotional truth and passion."[6]

The Truth

When asked why she wrote, Tan admitted that she did so for self-serving reasons. She writes for herself, because she enjoys stories and pretending. She also does it to keep her sanity, believing that if she did not write, she just might go crazy. Tan added, "Thus I write about questions that disturb me, images that mystify me, or memories that cause me anguish and pain. I write about secrets, lies, and contradictions, because within them are many kinds of truth. In other words, I write stories about life as I have misunderstood it."[7]

The world of words, the place Tan had turned to so many times as a child, began calling to her once again. It was time for her to return to her longtime dream of being an artist, only this time her canvas would be the blank page and her paintbrush a keyboard.

Amy Tan

Amy Tan and her mother, Daisy, in San Francisco

Chapter 6

From the time she was young, Tan was fascinated by words.

BECOMING A WRITER

After working at a number of different jobs, Tan could sense it was time to change direction. As her job working with children came to an end, she found herself renewing her

Amy Tan

passion for writing. In 1981, Tan established a business with a partner and began writing technical documents for large companies such as IBM, Pacific Bell, AT&T, and the Bank of America. She also wrote speeches for executives and salesmen. When Tan authored these documents, she wrote under pen names that did not sound like Chinese names, such as "May Brown." She was being paid well for her work and was even able to save enough money to buy her mother a house.

Tan's business was thriving, but she still was not happy. She was working 90 hours a week and did not get enough sleep at night. She had no social life and soon people she knew accused her of being a workaholic. It was confusing to her. She was making money and working with enjoyable clients, but she was still unhappy.

An Act of Faith

Tan still loves to read. She sees it as an act of faith and she hopes, as she reads, that she will find something unique or miraculous about life or even herself. If a writer and a reader can make that connection, she believes it is an act of magic. She wrote, "To me, that's the mystery and the wonder of both life and fiction—the connection between two unique individuals who discover in the end that they are more the same than they are different."[1]

Tan returned to the world of words when she established her business writing company.

Turning to Therapy

Tan put in more and more hours and still satisfaction escaped her. Instead, she felt trapped by her job. She did not always like what she was working on, and sometimes she felt pressure to take on more work than she could handle. She went into therapy searching for answers. When her psychiatrist fell asleep three different times during her counseling sessions, she knew it was time to quit therapy. Tan described,

> I would talk about feeling good and he'd fall asleep. But if I recalled something from my childhood that was traumatic, and I was crying, he was very attentive. And I thought, he's reinforcing me to be unhappy.[2]

But even though she quit going to therapy, Tan was still looking for happiness. She wanted to find something fulfilling.

Her business partner suggested that Tan stop writing and focus on the management part of the company. That only frustrated her more. One day in the mid-1980s, Tan's partner told her that her strength was in

The Invisible Force

Sometimes the stories that Tan wrote made her face the feelings she had about her own childhood and her relationship with her mother. When Tan wrote a scene about a Chinese-American girl who plays chess and the girl's mother, who was both her biggest supporter and strongest adversary, Tan ended up in tears. She realized that even though what she was writing was fictional and had never actually happened to her, it was the closest she had ever come to writing about her own life.

performing management details such as taking care of clients, giving estimates, going after contractors, and collecting bills. In Tan's opinion, those jobs were horrible. She would not tolerate them—she wanted to be a writer. However, her partner told her that writing was her weakest skill. They argued until Tan quit and got fired at the same time. When her partner asked her what she was going to do for work instead, Tan replied. "I'm going to freelance write." His response was less than enthusiastic. "Oh, fat chance," he stated. "You'll be lucky if you make a dime."[3]

That was the moment Tan knew she needed to shift her focus. Now she was absolutely determined to become a successful writer. She threw herself into her new path with renewed energy.

A Turn to Fiction

Although Tan had been toying with writing fiction while she was still immersed in her business writing company, she had not yet taken it seriously. That changed when she quit her job and one of her friends introduced her to a fiction writer. Tan showed her new friend some of the things she had written. Fortunately, this new friend loved

Amy Tan

Tan's stories. She was gentle in her critiquing but also quite supportive, so Tan decided to keep working on writing fiction.

After years of writing factual material, writing stories from her imagination was a new process for Tan. At first she tried writing about experiences that were completely unknown to her on a personal level. Tan stated,

> I wrote about a girl whose parents were educated, were professors at MIT. I tried to copy somebody's style that I thought was very clever. I thought I was clever enough to write as well as these people and I didn't realize that there is something called originality and your own voice.[4]

In 1985, Tan wrote a story called "Endgame" that lead to her joining a writer's group. She was also asked to attend her first writer's conference, the Squaw Valley Community of Writers. This group brings writers

At First

Like all good writers, Tan learned from her writing experiences and improved each time she wrote. However, looking back on her early writing sometimes makes her cringe. After reading over one of the original lines from her first draft of *The Joy Luck Club* that read, "That was my mental quandary in its nascent state," she immediately removed it, laughing that it was a line that she was barely able to pronounce.[5]

together for workshops, readings, and discussions. The goal of the group is to help the writers get their work published. The group has been meeting since 1969.

From this group, Tan met Molly Giles, another writer. Giles read some of Tan's work and encouraged her to find her own voice. She critiqued Tan by saying that her stories had potential, but not everything was working just yet. Her advice to Tan was to start over and work on making the characters more familiar. She also advised Tan to blend the stories. Those multiple stories would eventually become

> **Meet Molly Giles**
>
> In addition to being an inspiration and an editor to Tan, Molly Giles is a creative writing professor at the University of Arkansas in Fayetteville. Giles is also an author. Her short story collections are well-known. Her first collection, *Rough Translations*, was nominated for a Pulitzer Prize. In addition, she has been given the Flannery O'Connor Award for Short Fiction, the California Book Award for Fiction, and the Small Press Best Fiction/Short Story Award. Her second collection, *Creek Walk and Other Stories*, was named one of the *New York Times*' most notable books of 1997. She has received a National Endowment for the Arts award and has won two Pushcart Prizes.
>
> Giles's first novel, *Iron Shoes*, was published in 2001 by Simon & Schuster. It is a wryly humorous book about a woman who feels stuck in her life and unable to move in any direction. Her family is falling apart around her and she is searching for who she really is amidst the chaos. The book received good reviews.

Tan's first best-selling novel, *The Joy Luck Club*.

Finding Her Place

Tan loved the feedback—it was exactly what she needed. Instead of just saying her writing needed work, Giles pinpointed what Tan should do next. Tan began rewriting. Then, literary agent Sandra Dijkstra contacted her. Dijkstra had read one of Tan's stories, "Endgame," in a small literary magazine. The story was about a chess player who feels immense pressure from her mother. Dijkstra also read another of Tan's stories, "Waiting Between the Trees," and decided that she wanted to represent Tan as an author. About Dijkstra, Tan said,

> She pursued me and she kept saying, "You have to write more fiction." I said, "I can't pay you anything." She said, "I'm by commission. You don't have to pay

A Determined Agent

Sandra Dijkstra is a literary agent who works with more than 100 authors worldwide. She has been profiled in the *Los Angeles Times*, *Newsweek*, *Esquire*, *Publisher's Weekly*, and the *New York Observer*. Currently, Dijkstra is ranked as one of the nation's top five literary agents. When asked how she knows when she has found a true new talent, the agent responded, "One usually knows from the first sentence, in fiction, that one is in the presence of a talent, of a person with a voice and unique perspective on the world as well as his or her own special way of articulating that vision."[7]

anything until you sell anything. . . ." I thought, "Boy, is she dumb." She hounded me until I wrote a couple more stories and then she sold that as a collection called The Joy Luck Club.[6]

Little did Tan know that those stories would catapult her to fame in just a few short years.

Amy Tan

Tan was encouraged by others in the Squaw Valley Community of Writers.

Chapter 7

Amy Tan and her husband, Louis DeMattei, have been married since 1974.

Turning a Corner

Despite the inconsistent nature of Tan's relationship with her mother, Daisy, the two always loved each other. In 1986, Tan was frightened when her mother was put in the hospital after what appeared to be a heart attack. Tan made a promise that if her mother recovered, the two would take a trip to China together and spend time with Daisy's other daughters, who still lived there. Tan made another promise to herself as well, "If my mother lives, I will get to know her. I will ask her about her past and this time, I'll actually listen to what she has to say."[1]

Tan's mother did recover, and in 1987, mother and daughter left for a trip to China. They planned to stay with relatives, and brought along Robert Foothorap, a family friend and photographer. Tan admits he also came along to provide them with a fallback plan. If the trip was not going as well as she hoped, he was suddenly going to claim he needed to stay in a hotel. Tan's husband, Lou DeMattei, came along as well.

A New Perspective

This journey to Daisy's homeland truly was a turning point for Tan. She

Artistic Friends

Robert Foothorap has been a professional photographer since 1969. He uses a journalistic style of photography, and has taken an extensive amount of photographs of Amy Tan. Some of the photographs Foothorap has taken of Tan appear on the jackets of her books.

Foothorap is married to Gretchen Schields, a talented artist. Schields illustrated Tan's children's books and was the cover artist for a few of Tan's novels. Schields also worked with Tan on a PBS television show that aimed to inspire children to write their own stories.

suddenly saw her mother in an entirely new light. She saw Daisy not only as *her* mother, but the mother of other daughters. Tan listened as Daisy talked to these women as she often spoke to her, with criticism and correction—all delivered with love. It gave her comfort and helped her feel even more connected to her newly found half sisters. Tan explained,

> *I saw that my mother was a fascinating person formed by history in a particular time and place and that I wanted to know more about that time and place, as well as my mother. I wanted to know her history and there I was in the place where her history began.*[2]

The trip to China lasted for three weeks. This was intimidating to Tan because for many years, she had rarely spent more than a couple of hours with her mother at one time. It went well, however, and Tan had the opportunity to meet and spend time with more than 50 relatives during their travels.

Real History

Before her trip to China, Tan had not felt any real sense of history or connection to her heritage. She could imagine her past, but it was not until the visit to her family's homeland that she could imagine her ancestors and their roles in Chinese history. Until she experienced China, it had not seemed relevant to her life in the United States. Being in China and seeing its landscape, its geography, and its history changed that perspective. Tan found that China was surprisingly important to her.

Amy Tan

Tan stayed in Shanghai and Beijing during her trip to China in 1987.

When the group arrived, seven eager family members met them at the airport. Everyone piled into a van along with the luggage and took off on a harrowing ride through the streets of Shanghai. While Foothorap and DeMattei held on for dear life, Tan sat back and smiled. "I am an optimist," she wrote. "If we crash, I may not have to finish the novel I'm working on."[3] While they were in China,

Tan, DeMattei, Foothorap, and Daisy stayed with Tan's Aunt Elsie in an apartment in Shanghai. Later, they stayed at another aunt and uncle's place in Beijing.

One of Tan's biggest challenges during this visit was keeping up with the conversations around her. Although she knew some Chinese, the constant babbling stream coming from all directions as her relatives caught up with each other was overwhelming. She did a lot of smiling and nodding and hoped that it was the right response.

The trip to China was a very important event in Tan's life. The time spent with her mother was invaluable. In later years, Tan would be even more grateful for the trip with her mother. It would not be long before Daisy was diagnosed with Alzheimer's disease.

Speaking the Language

It is little wonder that Tan had trouble understanding the conversations around her when she sat with her family. Many of her relatives spoke Mandarin or Shanghainese.

Shanghainese is a spoken language only. It is used for everyday conversation but is not written down and is not used in schools. The Chinese government encourages Mandarin to be used, as it is considered more modern.

Amy Tan

Cultural Inspiration

The trip also proved to be an immense influence upon Tan's writing. For the first time, she was able to see her mother in her native environment. Tan was also able to see Chinese culture firsthand, and see her own place in it. She considered the trip to China as a turning point. The trip gave Tan the inspiration she needed to work on her manuscript and finish what would become her international best seller. After she returned, she wrote, "I couldn't

Living with Alzheimer's

As many as 5.2 million people in the United States suffer from Alzheimer's disease. In June 2008, the Centers for Disease Control and Prevention announced that Alzheimer's is the sixth leading cause of death in the United States.

Alzheimer's disease is a form of dementia. It is a condition that affects the brain so that memory is destroyed, and language and thought are impaired. This makes it difficult to learn, judge, communicate, and even manage a simple, daily routine. Although memory loss is often considered a normal part of aging, Alzheimer's is far more severe than occasionally forgetting a small detail. Family members can become strangers, and routine becomes mystery. Along with memory lapses, Alzheimer's can also cause anxiety, paranoia, and even hallucinations. The condition is also deadly because it destroys brain cells.

The causes of this disease are still unknown, although genetics, age, and the environment all seem to play a part. The cure for the condition is also unknown, although researchers have made many advances in their understanding of Alzheimer's. Groups such as the National Institutes of Health Alzheimer's Disease Prevention Initiative seek to understand, diagnose, and discover treatments for the disease.

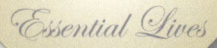

have written *The Joy Luck Club* without having been there, without having felt that spiritual sense of geography."[4]

When Tan returned from China, a surprise awaited her—one that would change her career as an author completely.

Amy Tan

Tan found a great deal of inspiration for her novels during her trip to China.

Chapter 8

Mahjong is a popular Chinese game.

FINDING JOY

Before Tan left for her journey with her mother, she had given *The Joy Luck Club* manuscript to her agent to show to a few publishers. When Tan returned, she was shocked to discover that the publisher G.P. Putnam's Sons had provided an advance of $50,000. As exciting as that was, it also put Tan under pressure. She had four months to get the manuscript polished and ready to turn in. When she was working on it, she had a routine. Tan explained,

> I'd light incense, put on certain music and start to imagine myself in another world. I conjured up people to come and tell me their stories. Then I'd enter that other world and hours would go by and I'd forget everything else.[1]

A Stunning Success

Amy made her deadline, and *The Joy Luck Club* was published in 1989. The story focuses on four women and their four daughters. One of the main themes is the difference between the mothers, who emigrated from China, and their daughters, who were born and raised in the

Writing for Children

Tan is the author of two popular books for children. *The Moon Lady*, a reworking of *The Joy Luck Club*, was published in 1995. It is based on the story of a grandmother telling her three granddaughters a tale of what happened to her on the evening of the Moon Festival when she was quite young. In 2001, Amy published *Sagwa, The Chinese Siamese Cat*. This is the tale of a Siamese cat that tells her kittens about one of their great ancestors. The book was turned into a children's television series.

United States. The mothers have many memories of China and never become entirely assimilated to the United States. The daughters, however, are fully immersed in U.S. culture and often dismiss their mothers as old-fashioned or embarrassing. Conflicts between mothers and daughters, as well as generational differences, are prevalent themes in Tan's writing.

The book was an amazing success and was on the *New York Times* Best Seller list for eight months. The book was also translated into 17 languages.

The Joy Luck Club on the Silver Screen

In 1993, *The Joy Luck Club* became a movie, with Amy Tan as screenwriter. Like the novel, the story is based on four women who are from China originally but live in San Francisco. They meet on a regular basis to play the game mahjong. Mahjong is a Chinese game for four players and is played with tiles. Each character in the movie has a daughter whom they worry about, love, and discuss.

Casting was challenging, as the movie goes forward and backward in time. It took a total of 15 actresses to play the primary parts. The script called for 60 actors with speaking parts, and 50 of those parts were for women. Director Wayne Wang also wanted to find actors who spoke Mandarin Chinese, so that scenes taking place in China would not have to be dubbed over with voice actors. Instead, he used subtitles during the scenes that include Chinese dialogue. Wang described the confusion. "It was like a puzzle," he said. "Right from the start, I knew that if we cast this movie right, my job would be half done. And if we didn't, I would be in a lot of trouble."[2] The film received excellent reviews overall and was considered for several awards, including a British Academy of Film and Television Arts Award and Writers Guild Award.

The paperback rights sold for $1.23 million. *The Joy Luck Club* became one of the top five finalists for that year's National Book Award.

Tan was stunned by the book's reception. She attributed its success to pure luck, like winning the lottery. She owes much of the book's popularity, she believes, to the fact that she wrote about emotions and conflicts that many people go through. Because of this, she believes the book struck a chord with readers. She also thinks that she just happened to be in the right place at the right time and happened to meet the right people.

Finding an Answer

In the midst of all the success over her first book, Tan found herself struggling with her emotions. It did not take her long to realize that she was battling a serious case of depression. She spent the entire day

Living with Depression

According to the World Health Organization, depression affects approximately 121 million people in the world. Depression tends to affect women more than men. However, the fastest-growing group of people suffering from some form of depression is children. More than three-quarters of the people who have the condition do not receive any treatment. Experts predict that by the year 2020, depression will be the second largest killer in the United States, only surpassed by heart disease.

Amy Tan, actress Annette Bening, and director Wayne Wang at the screening of The Joy Luck Club in 1993.

of her publication party for *The Joy Luck Club* crying. "I was scared out of my mind that my life was changing and it was out of my control and I didn't know why it was happening."³

She recognized the symptoms of depression because she had seen them for so long in her mother and through tales of her grandmother. While she believes that some of her depression is based on biochemistry, or the chemicals in her brain, she thinks genetics play a large role as well. For a long time, Tan did not do anything to address or fix how she was feeling. Like many other people, she was reluctant to take medication that altered her mood and her thinking processes. As a writer, the thought of changing those things truly concerned her.

Tan's condition did not improve when her second book, *The Kitchen God's Wife*, came out. Tan broke out in hives and claimed, "I couldn't sleep at night. I broke three teeth grinding my teeth. I had backaches . . . I was a wreck!"[4]

Getting Help

When the film version of *The Joy Luck Club* premiered in 1993, Tan was crashing emotionally. Her mother was very proud of her, something

A Possible Solution

There are many different antidepressants in today's marketplace. Most of these medications work by making certain essential natural chemicals more available for the brain to use. These are typically divided into categories based on which specific brain chemicals they affect. Although many of them can be quite helpful, each has a number of side effects including insomnia, nausea, weight gain, headaches, anxiety, and dry mouth.

Tan had longed for since she was young. But she explained, "Everything should have been the formula for somebody being extremely happy. But I cried all day. I felt suicidal. I wanted to jump off the roof."[5]

Tan finally realized that she could not continue to ignore these feelings. She began taking a prescription drug to help her cope with her depression. The drug helped. She was relieved to discover that it did not change who she was, but instead helped treat her depression and helped her feel more balanced.

Losing Family and Friends

In 1999, Daisy Tan's health was failing. She died in her San Francisco home on November 22, 1999, at the age of 83. Before she died, she revealed something that mystified Tan. She told her daughter that her real name was Li Bingzi. When Daisy revealed her real name, it reminded Tan that her mother was a woman with many secrets who had lived an extraordinary life.

Within two weeks, Tan's editor and friend Faith Sale also died. She had been suffering from cancer.

At the time, Tan was writing *The Bonesetter's Daughter*, but after her mother passed away, she began

Amy Tan

writing the story all over again. She explained,

> I couldn't write the real story until after my mother had gone because I felt that by not finishing it both she and my editor would have to stay just because I needed them. When they died two weeks apart, I almost threw the book away because it seemed so meaningless compared to what I'd gone through. But then I also felt that I had two people to help me, that I had a ghost writer and a ghost editor.[6]

But Tan kept working on *The Bonesetter's Daughter*, and it was published in 2001. Like her other writings, it contains a great deal of culture, tradition, family secrets, and a focus on the clash between "old" and "new." Set in current-day San Francisco and a Chinese village, the novel centers on the relationships between a mother and her daughter. The book was well received and praised by critics and

Thankfulness

In the acknowledgements in *The Bonesetter's Daughter*, Tan thanks her late editor, Faith Sale, for all her help. Tan writes, "To my astonishment, she could always sense the difference between what I was trying to write and what I wanted to write. She promised she would see me through this book, and though she died before I finished, I believe she kept her promise."[7]

fans. Tan embarked on a 22-city book tour after its publication. But Tan did not rest after she wrote *The Bonesetter's Daughter*. She stated that an hour after she finished the manuscript for the book, she had started writing her next novel.

Amy Tan

Amy Tan's editor, Faith Sale, with Daisy Tan in New York City

Chapter 9

In addition to her writing, Amy Tan attends public events and awards ceremonies focused on the arts.

Keeping Up, Looking Forward

Since the publication of *The Joy Luck Club*, Amy Tan has continued to please thousands of readers with her novels, short stories, and essays. With the publication of her two books for children, she has been able to entertain young readers as well. Tan has also translated her talents into art forms other than writing. She continues to play music with her band of authors, the Rock Bottom Remainders. The group tours together once a year.

In 2003, Tan received some scary news about her health. Earlier that year, she had been having hallucinations when she woke from sleeping. She began behaving oddly and then having no memory of it. She began having soreness in her back and neck, and sometimes she had trouble sleeping. Tan's experiences frightened her, but not knowing what caused them was worse.

As this continued, it became more difficult for her to concentrate when she tried to write. By the third or fourth page, she would forget what she had written and had to start all over again. When talking with

Making Music

The Rock Bottom Remainders is a band made up of some of the United States' most popular and well-known authors. In addition to Amy Tan, members include Dave Barry, Stephen King, Roy Blount Jr., Matt Groening, Mitch Albom, Scott Turow, and Ridley Pearson.

The group first performed in 1992 at the American Booksellers Association convention in Anaheim, California. They do not have any records, music videos, or Grammy nominations, but they have raised millions of dollars for literacy groups.

friends, she struggled to follow the conversation. She nodded and laughed whenever everyone else did and hoped that no one noticed that she was lost.

Tan finally met with a psychiatrist who recommended a full medical examination. She had a magnetic resonance imaging (MRI) and two computerized axial tomography (CAT) scans. Her results came back normal. She consulted an endocrinologist, a cardiologist, and an orthopedic surgeon. No one had any answers. After doing some research of her own, she suspected that she might have Lyme disease, which is caused by a tick bite. Tan had seen an unusual rash on her skin, with a tiny blood blister in the middle. The blister went away, but the rash remained for about a month. Tan wondered if the strange rash was related to the hallucinations and the physical symptoms she had experienced.

Tan was diagnosed with late-stage Lyme disease. The diagnosis explained her symptoms of hair loss, memory loss, replacing words with gibberish when speaking, vertigo, joint pain, numbness, and fatigue. She was treated with a course of antibiotics. Although they helped, Tan still suffers from some of the disease's effects today.

Amy Tan

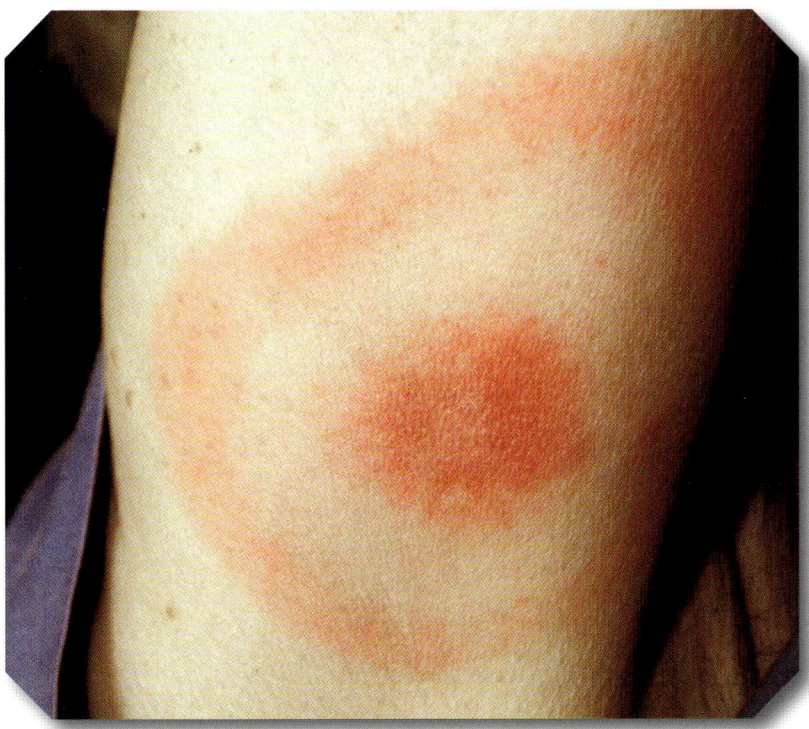

Some tick bites result in a rash that resembles a bull's-eye. This can be a sign of Lyme disease.

Inspiring Others

It is clear that Tan not only pleases readers with her writing. In addition to providing the material for many types of artistic enjoyment, such as a movie and an opera, Tan also has been inspirational to other writers. After the publication of *The Joy Luck Club*, other Asian-American authors began to be published. Some say that Tan paved the way and sparked a public interest in Asian culture and literature. While this pleases Tan, it also embarrasses her somewhat. She tends to think of herself more as a writer than an Asian-American writer. Although her heritage is important to her, it is not all there is to know about her.

Internet Confusion

Tan also took time to look herself up on the Internet. She was so taken aback by all the mistakes she saw written about her life that she wrote an essay called "Persona Errata" to make sure the truth was told. While she was looking on the Internet, she found

---

Coping with Lyme Disease

Approximately 25,000 cases of Lyme disease are reported in the United States each year. Lyme disease is caused by the Borrelia burgdorferi bacterium, which is carried by an infected tick. When the tick bites a human, the bacterium is transferred. Typically, this bite will cause a skin rash that looks like a bull's-eye, with a round red ring and a paler ring inside it. Some bites, however, are so small that the rash never appears or is too tiny to notice. Along with the rash, there are a series of symptoms including headaches, sore throat, stiff neck, fever, muscle aches, and fatigue.

Even without treatment, the symptoms may disappear but are followed by more serious complication months or years later. Muscle and joint pain are common. Additional symptoms include numbness, tingling sensations in the extremities, Bell's palsy (the loss of control of one or both sides of the face), extreme fatigue, and depression. Heart, eye, respiratory, and gastrointestinal problems can develop as well. Typical treatment is a series of antibiotics. The earlier the medication is taken, the better the chance of it helping an infected person feel better.

out that for a mere $25.99, a staff of writing professionals could provide students with essays, research papers, and even entire dissertations on Amy Tan. She wrote,

> How dismal to think I can be instantly summed up for only $25.99. These papers could not possibly be correct. I've paid psychiatrists $200 for fifty minutes many times over, and I still don't understand who I am.[1]

On her personal Web site, Tan has expressed frustration with the media and its portrayal of her. She does not always enjoy being in the spotlight and has been annoyed by the liberties some interviewers take when writing about her. In other cases, some articles and sites on the Internet give information that is false. For example, one site stated that she had won the Nobel Prize for Literature, which is not true. Tan also becomes upset when writers refer to DeMattei

Purgatory

Book tours can be exhausting and Tan knows the drill well. Each day, she would wake up and have to remember what city she was in. "Purgatory is one long airplane trip with only memories of hotel rooms," she stated. As she phrased it, book tours are like "punishment for writing a book."[2]

as her "current husband." She has only been married once—to DeMattei in 1974—and the couple remains married.

Recent Writing

Tan's latest book, *Saving Fish from Drowning*, published in 2005, was a distinct departure from her earlier novels. It does not center on the history and relationships of Asian-American families or on Tan's personal experiences.

The humorous story is narrated in the voice of Bibi Chen, an outspoken and pushy ghost, and is about a group of people who travel from San Francisco to Burma. The group gets lost in the jungle on Christmas morning. Tan's characters include a divorced British dog trainer, a bamboo grower and his sulky teenage son, a left-wing activist, and a behavioral psychologist. By the end of the story, all the different

Keeping Silent

In interviews, Tan is often asked to discuss the book she is currently working on, but she refuses. "I never talk about what a new book is about as it will leave me," she said. "There is a story in Chinese where a man goes to a magical place and is overwhelmed by the beauty and the peace. He has to leave and they tell him that if he tells anyone where this place is he will never find it again. That is the metaphor for writing. You are in a secret place and discovering it but once you tell people it is gone."[3]

personalities have become friends with one another.

New Projects

Tan is unsure what projects she will take on in the future. Maintaining her health will remain a high priority. She also will watch how audiences respond to her stories told through an operatic presentation.

When asked if there was anything else in life that she wanted to do but had not had the opportunity yet, Tan replied,

> There are so many things I want to do. I would like to go trekking into Nepal. I would like to write a song. I would like to breed Yorkies. Sometimes I think I would like to be an interior decorator. There are so many things but the nice thing about being a writer is if I can't do all of those things, all I have to do is imagine them and put them in a story. That's second place but it's pretty good.[4]

Lilli and Bubba

DeMattei and Tan decided not to have children. But they do dote on their two tiny dogs, Lilliput and Bubba. In between books, these two dogs have provided Tan with endless company and entertainment. "My saving grace and chief distraction have been my dogs, two travel-sized Yorkshire terriers . . . who weigh a combined total of 5 ½ pounds," she said. "They adore me no matter how many bad sentences I write, no matter how much I have not accomplished. They sit on my lap as I work and we spend an awful lot of time reading various AOL message boards related to dogs."[5] In 2008, Bubba died and Tan got a new puppy named King Bombo.

And when asked how she hopes to be remembered, Tan would like people to say that "she had an extraordinary amount of good luck and she shared it with others."[6]

Amy Tan

Tan continues to play music with the Rock Bottom Remainders to raise support for literacy groups.

Timeline

1952
Amy Tan is born in Oakland, California, on February 19.

1960
Tan's first essay is published in the Santa Rosa *Press Democrat*.

1967
Tan's father dies of a brain tumor.

1973
Tan earns a master's degree from San Jose State University.

1974
Tan marries Louis DeMattei on April 6.

1976
Tan's friend Pete is murdered.

Amy Tan

1968
Tan's older brother, Peter, dies of a brain tumor. The family moves to Switzerland.

1969
Tan graduates from Institut Monte Rosa Internationale High School and the family returns to the United States.

1972
Tan graduates with honors from San Jose State University.

1976–1981
Tan works for the Alameda County Association for Retarded Citizens.

1981
Tan begins her own business writing company.

1986
Sandra Dijkstra becomes Tan's book agent and encourages her to write more fiction.

Timeline

1987
Tan, DeMattei, Tan's mother Daisy, and friend Robert Foothorap travel to China.

1989
The Joy Luck Club is published.

1991
The Kitchen God's Wife is published.

2001
The Bonesetter's Daughter is published.

2003
The Opposite of Fate is published. Tan is diagnosed with Lyme disease.

Amy Tan

1993
The film version of *The Joy Luck Club* premieres.

1995
The Hundred Secret Senses is published.

1999
Tan's mother and editor pass away within two weeks of each other.

2005
Saving Fish from Drowning is published.

2008
The Bonesetter's Daughter is made into an opera.

Essential Facts

Date of Birth
February 19, 1952

Place of Birth
Oakland, California

Parents
John and Daisy Tan

Education
- Institut Monte Rosa Internationale High School in Switzerland
- Linfield College in Oregon
- San Jose City College and San Jose State University in California

Marriage
Louis DeMattei (April 6, 1974)

Children
None

Career Highlights
- Tan's books include *The Joy Luck Club*, *The Kitchen God's Wife*, *The Bonesetter's Daughter*, and *Saving Fish from Drowning*.
- Tan was the screenwriter for the 1993 movie version of *The Joy Luck Club*.

- Tan's novel *The Bonesetter's Daughter* was made into an opera.
- Tan has also written two children's books.

Societal Contribution

Audiences around the world have enjoyed Tan's stories. Her stories have been made into movies, operas, and television shows. Tan also paved the way for other Asian-American authors to have their work published. Tan offers much advice to aspiring authors on how they can improve their writing.

Conflicts

- Tan's relationship with her mother, Daisy, was rocky at times. Daisy held many Chinese beliefs and practiced Chinese traditions that sometimes embarrassed or confused Tan as a child.
- Tan suffers from Lyme disease. Although she receives treatment for the disease, she still battles its side effects.

Quote

"To me, that's the mystery and the wonder of both life and fiction—the connection between two unique individuals who discover in the end that they are more the same than they are different."—*Amy Tan*, The Opposite of Fate

Additional Resources

Select Bibliography

Giles, Gretchen. "Bay Area author Amy Tan talks about fame and phantoms." *Sonoma Independent*. 14 Dec. 1995. <http://www.metroactive.com/papers/sonoma/12.14.95/tan-9550.html>.

Gray, Paul, and Andrea Sachs. "The Joys and Sorrows of Amy Tan." *Time*. 11 Feb. 2001. <http://www.time.com/time/magazine/article/0,9171,999251,00.html>.

Huntley, E. D. *Amy Tan: A Critical Companion*. Westport, CT: Greenwood Press, 1998.

Loose, Cindy. "Amy Tan's San Francisco: Dim Sum and then Some." *Washingtonpost.com*. 21 Jan. 2007. <http://www.washingtonpost.com/wp-dyn/content/article/2007/01/19/AR2007011900541_pf.html>.

Lyall, Sarah. "At Home with Amy Tan: In the Country of the Spirits." *New York Times*. 28 Dec. 1995. <http://www.nytimes.com/books/01/02/18/specials/tan-home.html>.

Tan, Amy. *The Opposite of Fate*. New York: Putnam Books, 2003.

Further Reading

Adams, Bella. *Amy Tan*. Manchester, UK: Manchester University Press, 2005.

Shea, Renee H., and Deborah Wilchek. *Amy Tan in the Classroom: The Art of Invisible Strength*. Urbana, IL: National Council of Teachers of English, 2005.

Shields, Charles. *Amy Tan*. New York: Chelsea House Publications, 2001.

Smith, Ken. *Fate! Luck! Chance! Amy Tan, Stewart Wallace, and the Making of the Bonesetter's Daughter*. San Francisco, CA: Chronicle Books, 2008.

Web Links

To learn more about Amy Tan, visit ABDO Publishing Company online at **www.abdopublishing.com**. Web sites about Amy Tan are featured on our Book Links page. These links are routinely monitored and updated to provide the most current information available.

Places to Visit

Chinese Culture Center of San Francisco
750 Kearny Street, Third Floor, San Francisco, CA 94108
415–986–1822
http://c-c-c.org
The Chinese Culture Center of San Francisco seeks to cultivate an appreciation of Chinese history, culture, and art. Past exhibitions include collections of traditional Chinese games, puzzles, architecture, and activist artwork.

San Francisco's Chinatown
Downtown San Francisco, CA
www.sfgov.org/site/planning_index.asp?id=41403
San Francisco's Chinatown is the largest community of Chinese people on the West Coast. San Francisco's Chinatown includes restaurants, shops, bakeries, and points of cultural interest. Traditional Chinese festivals are celebrated throughout the year.

Glossary

adversary
   An enemy.

Alzheimer's disease
   A fatal brain disorder that destroys brain cells and causes memory loss.

aspire
   To desire or seek after something.

Bell's palsy
   A condition that causes facial paralysis.

censorship
   To exclude or remove books and materials that one thinks are offensive or inappropriate.

commission
   A fee that is paid to an agent when the agent sells a piece of writing.

conjured
   Summoned or invoked.

convulsions
   Spasms.

cynic
   A person who is distrustful or doubtful of human nature.

divinity school
   A religious school for students who intend to work in religious ministry.

endearing
   Beloved or admired.

ethereal
   Light, airy, or intangible.

fatigue
   Exhaustion or extreme tiredness.

freelancer
   A writer who works independently.

hallucination
    A vision of something that is not actually there.

incense
    A material that produces a fragrance when burned.

insomnia
    Inability to sleep.

linguistics
    The study of language and human speech.

literacy
    The state of being able to read and write.

Lyme disease
    A bacterial infection caused by tick bites that causes flu-like symptoms.

migrating
    Moving to another country.

mortician
    A person who prepares a dead body and arranges funerals.

nascent
    Newly born or newly existent.

premonition
    A warning.

prologue
    In an opera, an introduction before the first act.

quandary
    A state of being confused or in doubt.

steeped
    To be saturated.

vertigo
    A state of dizziness.

wryly
    Cleverly or ironically.

Source Notes

Chapter 1. From Page to Stage
1. Steven Winn. "Amy Tan's opera: 'The Bonesetter's Daughter.'" *SFGate.com*. 24 Aug. 2008. 22 Oct. 2008 <http://www.sfgate.com/cgi-bin/article.cgi?f=/c/a/2008/08/22/PKEK12B8K1.DTL>.
2. Joshua Kosman. "Opera review: 'Bonesetter's Daughter.'" *SFGate.com*. 15 Sept. 2008. 12 Jan. 2009 <http://www.sfgate.com/cgi-bin/article.cgi?f=/c/a/2008/09/15/DDGV12TU9R.DTL>.
3. Bella Adams. *Amy Tan*. Manchester, UK: Manchester University Press, 2005. 2.
4. Amy Tan. *The Opposite of Fate*. New York: Putnam Books, 2003. 266.

Chapter 2. Fitting In
1. Cindy Loose. "Amy Tan's San Francisco: Dim Sum and then Some." *Washingtonpost.com*. 21 Jan. 2007. 25 Sept. 2008 <http://www.washingtonpost.com/wp-dyn/content/article/2007/01/19/AR2007011900541_pf.html>.
2. Amy Tan. *The Opposite of Fate*. New York: Putnam Books, 2003. 125.
3. Ibid. 127.
4. Ibid. 126.
5. "Amy Tan Interview." *Academy of Achievement*. 11 Sept. 2008 <http://www.achievement.org/autodoc/page/tan0int-1>.

Chapter 3. Growing Up
1. "Amy Tan Interview." *Academy of Achievement*. 20 Sept. 2008 <http://www.achievement.org/autodoc/page/tan0int-1>.
2. "Author Talk: Amy Tan." *The Book Reporter*. Nov. 2005. 25 Sept. 2008 <http://www.bookreporter.com/authors/au-tan-amy.asp>.
3. "Amy Tan Interview." *Academy of Achievement*. 20 Sept. 2008 <http://www.achievement.org/autodoc/page/tan0int-1>.
4. Ibid.
5. Ibid.

6. Amy Tan. *The Opposite of Fate*. New York: Putnam Books, 2003. 269.
7. "Amy Tan Interview." *Academy of Achievement*. 20 Sept. 2008 <http://www.achievement.org/autodoc/page/tan0int-1>.

Chapter 4. Losing Loved Ones
1. Bel Mooney. "Mixing It." *New Internationalist*. Aug. 2004. 22 Sept. 2008 <http://www.newint.org/features/2004/08/01/devout-scepticism/>.
2. Ibid.
3. "Amy Tan Interview." *Academy of Achievement*. 20 Sept. 2008 <http://www.achievement.org/autodoc/page/tan0int-1>.
4. Gretchen Giles. "Bay Area author Amy Tan talks about fame and phantoms." *Sonoma Independent*. 14 Dec. 1995. 6 Oct. 2008 <http://www.metroactive.com/papers/sonoma/12.14.95/tan-9550.html>.
5. "Amy Tan Interview." *Academy of Achievement*. 20 Sept. 2008 <http://www.achievement.org/autodoc/page/tan0int-1>.
6. Sarah Lyall. "At Home with Amy Tan: In the Country of the Spirits." *New York Times*. 28 Dec. 1995. 6 Oct. 2008 <http://query.nytimes.com/gst/fullpage.html?res=9802EFDE1239F93BA15751C1A963958260&partner=rssnyt&emc=rss>.
7. Amy Tan. *The Opposite of Fate*. New York: Putnam Books, 2003. 213.

Chapter 5. Purpose through Loss
1. "Amy Tan Interview." *Academy of Achievement*. 20 Sept. 2008 <http://www.achievement.org/autodoc/page/tan0int-1>.
2. Amy Tan. *The Opposite of Fate*. New York: Putnam Books, 2003. 49.
3. Ibid. 55.
4. Ibid. 56.
5. "Amy Tan Interview." *Academy of Achievement*. 20 Sept. 2008 <http://www.achievement.org/autodoc/page/tan0int-1>.

Source Notes Continued

6. Sarah Lyall. "At Home with Amy Tan: In the Country of the Spirits." *New York Times*. 28 Dec. 1995. 6 Oct. 2008 <http://nytimes.com/books/01/02/18/specials/tan-home.html>.
7. Amy Tan. *The Opposite of Fate*. New York: Putnam Books, 2003. 304–305.

Chapter 6. Becoming a Writer
1. Amy Tan. *The Opposite of Fate*. New York: Putnam Books, 2003. 323.
2. David Streitfeld. "The 'Luck' of Amy Tan." *The Washington Post*. 8 Oct. 1989. 10 Nov. 2008 <http://davidstreitfeld.com/archive/writers/amytan.html#>.
3. "Amy Tan Interview." *Academy of Achievement*. 20 Sept. 2008 <http://www.achievement.org/autodoc/page/tan0int-1>.
4. Ibid.
5. Amy Tan. *The Opposite of Fate*. New York: Putnam Books, 2003. 278.
6. "Amy Tan Interview." *Academy of Achievement*. 20 Sept. 2008 <http://www.achievement.org/autodoc/page/tan0int-1>.
7. Berrill Hall Bray. "Sandra Dijkstra Works for Authors, Not for Publishers." *Women on Writing*. 1 Oct. 2008 <http://wow-womenonwriting.com/3-sandradijkstra.php>.

Chapter 7. Turning a Corner
1. Amy Tan. *The Opposite of Fate*. New York: Putnam Books, 2003. 358.
2. "Author Talk: Amy Tan." *The Book Reporter*. Nov. 2005. 25 Sept. 2008 <http://www.bookreporter.com/authors/au-tan-amy.asp>.
3. Amy Tan. *The Opposite of Fate*. New York: Putnam Books, 2003. 157.
4. "Amy Tan Interview." *Academy of Achievement*. 20 Sept. 2008 <http://www.achievement.org/autodoc/page/tan0int-1>.

Chapter 8. Finding Joy
1. E. D. Huntley. *Amy Tan: A Critical Companion*. Westport. CT: Greenwood Press, 1998. 14.

2. Mimi Avins. "How to Tell the Players in the 'The Joy Luck Club.'" *New York Times*. 5 Sept. 1993. 6 Oct. 2008 <http://nytimes.com/books/01/02/18/specials/tan-players.html>.
3. "Amy Tan Interview." *Academy of Achievement*. 20 Sept. 2008 <http://www.achievement.org/autodoc/page/tan0int-1>.
4. Ibid.
5. Paul Gray and Andrea Sachs. "The Joys and Sorrows of Amy Tan." *Time*. 19 Feb. 2001. 29 Sept. 2008 <http://www.time.com/time/magazine/article/0,9171,999251,00.html>.
6. "Author Talk: Amy Tan." *The Book Reporter*. Nov. 2005. 25 Sept. 2008 <http://www.bookreporter.com/authors/au-tan-amy.asp>.
7. Amy Tan. *The Bonesetter's Daughter*. New York: Putnam Books, 2001. N. pag.

Chapter 9. Keeping Up, Looking Forward
1. Amy Tan. *The Opposite of Fate*. New York: Putnam Books, 2003. 116.
2. Gretchen Giles. "Bay Area author Amy Tan talks about fame and phantoms." *Sonoma Independent*. 14 Dec. 1995. 25 Sept. 2008 <http://www.metroactive.com/papers/sonoma/12.14.95/tan-9550.html>.
3. Belinda Goldsmith. "Joy Luck Club author writing again as health improves." *New Zealand Herald*. 27 June 2007. 29 Sept. 2008 <http://www.nzherald.co.nz/lifestyle/news/article.cfm?c_id=6&objectid=10448256>.
4. "Amy Tan Interview." *Academy of Achievement*. 20 Sept. 2008 <http://www.achievement.org/autodoc/page/tan0int-1>.
5. "Author Talk: Amy Tan." *The Book Reporter*. Nov. 2005. 25 Sept. 2008 <http://www.bookreporter.com/authors/au-tan-amy.asp>.
6. Mimi Towle. "Amy Tan." *Marin Magazine*. Sept. 2008. 26 Sept. 2008 <http://www.marinmagazine.com/Marin-Magazine/September-2008/Amy-Tan/>.

Index

Alameda County Association for Retarded Citizens, 54
Alzheimer's disease, 72, 73
ancestors, 21, 26–27, 37, 38, 70, 77

blind date, 46, 50
Bonesetter's Daughter, The (novel), 7, 10, 82–84
Bonesetter's Daughter, The (opera), 6–10

Chinatown, 18
CliffsNotes, 11
computerized axial tomography, 88
"Confessions," 43

DeMattei, Louis, 49–51, 69, 71, 91–92, 93
Dijkstra, Sandra, 65

"Endgame," 63, 65

feng shui, 40
Foothorap, Robert, 69, 71
Franz (boyfriend), 42–43, 45, 48

G.P. Putnam's Sons, 77
geomancers, 39–40
Giles, Molly, 64–65

Hundred Secret Senses, The, 10

immigrants, 10, 18
Institut Monte Rosa Internationale High School, 44, 45

Joy Luck Club, The (film), 78, 81
Joy Luck Club, The (novel), 10, 11, 63, 65–66, 74, 76–80, 86, 89

Kitchen God's Wife, The, 10, 11, 81

Linfield College, 45, 46, 49, 50
literary critics, 11, 12–13, 83
literary themes
  identity crisis, 13, 78
  mother-daughter relationships, 61, 77–78, 83
  travel, 92–93

magnetic resonance imaging, 88
mahjong, 78
Mandarin, 33, 72, 78
marijuana, 45
Massachusetts Institute of Technology, 27, 28
Montreux, Switzerland, 41, 44
Moon Lady, The, 77

Opposite of Fate: A Book of Musings, The, 10, 11, 12

"Persona Errata," 90–91
Pete (friend), 50–54
police, 44–45, 51

"Question of Fate, A," 51–52

Rock Bottom Remainders, The, 87

Sagwa, The Chinese Siamese Cat, 77
San Jose City College, 46
San Jose State University, 49
Santa Rosa *Press Democrat*, 32
Saving Fish from Drowning, 10, 92–93
Schields, Gretchen, 69
Shanghainese, 33, 72
Squaw Valley Community of Writers, 63–64

Tan, Amy
  childhood, 16–25, 28–34
  Chinese sisters, 40–41, 70
  death of brother and father, 37–38
  depression, 79–82
  language development consultant, 53–55
  Lyme disease, 87–88, 90
  marriage, 49, 92
  moving, 22, 39–41, 42, 46
  pressure from parents, 11, 28–31
  rebellion, 42–46, 48–49
  religious influences, 29, 32, 36–37
  suicidal thoughts, 23, 82

  therapy, 60–61
  trip to China, 69–74
  writing business, 59–62
  writing routine, 77
Tan, Daisy (mother)
  Alzheimer's disease, 72
  Chinese heritage, 17, 18, 20–21
  death, 82–83
  faith, 37–38
  marriage, 27–28
  moving, 38–41
  relationship with Amy, 12–13, 23, 29, 42–46, 48–49, 55, 61, 68, 81
  storytelling, 29, 33, 55
  trip to China, 69–73
Tan, John (brother), 19, 28, 39
Tan, John (father), 27–29, 36–38
Tan, Peter (brother), 19, 28, 37–38
traditions, 10, 20–21, 83

University of California Berkeley, 49, 50

Wallace, Stephen, 7–8, 10
Wang, Wayne, 78
War Memorial Opera House, 7

About the Author

Tamra Orr is the author of more than 150 nonfiction books and biographies. Orr graduated from Ball State University in 1982 with a degree in English and Secondary Education. She lives in the Pacific Northwest with her husband, four children, one dog, and one cat. When she is not writing a book, she is reading one. Being able to write about Amy Tan, one of her favorite authors, was a special treat for her.

Photo Credits

Will Ragozzino/Getty Images, cover; Terrence McCarthy, 6; Joe Tabacca/AP Images, 9; Lawrence Lucier/Stringer/Getty Images, 15; Copyright © by Amy Tan. Reprinted by permission of the author and the Sandra Dijkstra Literary Agency, 16, 26, 30, 35, 36, 48, 85; Hywit Dimyadi/iStock Photo, 20; Bob Klein/AP Images, 25; iStock Photo, 39; Bogdan Lazar/iStock Photo, 47; Cheng Chang/iStock Photo, 52; Jim McHugh, 57, 68; Amy/Sussman/Stringer/Getty Images, 58; Tammie Arroyo/Getty Images, 60; Suzie Maeder/Lebrecht Music & Arts/Corbis, 67; Red Line Editorial, 71; Ivor Clarke/iStock Photo, 75; Louis Aguinaldo/iStock Photo, 76; Michael Tweed/AP Images, 80; Amy Tierney/WireImage/Getty Images, 86; James Gathany/AP Images, 89; Katy Winn/Corbis, 95